Singer's Pop/Rock Fake Book

EDITION

D0707684

This publication is not for sale in
the EU and/or Australia
or New Zealand.

ISBN 0-7935-5990-1

HAL•LEONARD®
CORPORATION
7777 W. BLUEMOUND RD. P.O. BOX 13819 MILWAUKEE, WI 53213

CONTENTS

ALL I NEED IS A MIRACLE

Words and Music by CHRISTOPHER NEIL
and MICHAEL RUTHERFORD

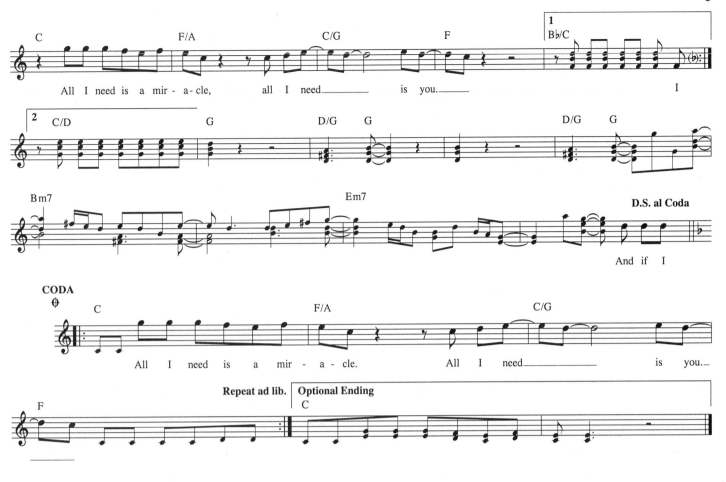

All I need is a mir-a-cle, all I need is you. I

C/D G D/G G D/G G

Bm7 Em7 D.S. al Coda

And if I

CODA

All I need is a mir-a-cle. All I need is you.

Repeat ad lib. | Optional Ending

BABY, WHAT YOU WANT ME TO DO

Words and Music by
JIMMY REED

Shuffle Blues

1. You got me run-nin', you got me hid-in', you got me
up, go-in' down, go-in'
peep-in', got me hid-in', got me

run, hide, hide, run, an - y way you wan-na let it roll. Yeah, yeah,
up, down, down, up, an - y way you wan-na let it roll.
peep, hide, hide, peep, an - y way you wan-na let it roll.

yeah. You got me do-in' what you want me, ba - by, why you wan-na let

1, 2 Repeat ad lib.; instrumental verses may be added | Last time

E E/G# A A#dim7 B7   E E/G# A A#dim7 B7 E E7

go?   2. Go-in'
3. Got me
go?

BEST OF MY LOVE

Words and Music by JOHN DAVID SOUTHER,
DON HENLEY and GLENN FREY

Moderately slow

Ev-er-y night__ I'm ly-in' in bed,__ hold-in' you close__ in my dreams;__

think-in' a-bout__ all the things that we__ said__ and com-in' a-part__ at the seams.__

We try to talk it o-ver but the words come out__ too__ rough;__ I

know you were try-in' to give me the best__ of your__ love.

Beau-ti-ful fac-es, loud, emp-ty plac-es— look at the way that we live,__

wast-in' our time__ on cheap talk and wine__ left us so lit-tle to give.__ That

(Ooh)__ (Ooh)__

same old__ crowd__ was like a cold dark cloud__ that we could nev-er rise a-bove,__

but here in my heart__ I give you the best__ of my__ love.

Oh,__ sweet dar-lin,

you get the best of my__ love,

(you get the best of my

7

BEAUTIFUL IN MY EYES

Words and Music by
JOSHUA KADISON

BLACKBIRD

Words and Music by JOHN LENNON
and PAUL McCARTNEY

BLUE SUEDE SHOES

Words and Music by
CARL LEE PERKINS

Bright tempo (not too fast)

Well, it's one for the mon- ey, two for the show, three to get read- y, now go, cat, go. But,

don't you step on my blue suede shoes. You can

do an- y- thing,_ but lay off of my blue suede shoes.__ Well, you can

knock me down,_ step on my face,_ slan- der my name all o- ver the place;-
burn my house,_ steal_ my car,_ drink_ my ci- der from my old_ fruit jar.__

do an- y- thing that you want to do,_ but uh- uh, hon- ey, lay off of my shoes._

Don't you step on my blue suede shoes. You can do an- y- thing_ but lay

off of my blue suede shoes._____ Well, you can shoes._____

BROWN EYED GIRL

Words and Music by
VAN MORRISON

BUILD ME UP, BUTTERCUP

Words and Music by TONY McCAULEY
and MICHAEL D'ABO

Can You Feel the Love Tonight

from Walt Disney Pictures' THE LION KING

Music by ELTON JOHN
Lyrics by TIM RICE

Pop Ballad

There's a calm sur-ren-der to the rush of day,— when the heat of the roll-ing world
There's a time for ev-'ry-one, if they on-ly learn— that the twist-ing ka-lei-do-scope

can be turned a-way. An en-chant-ed mo-ment, and it sees— me through.
moves us all— in turn. There's a rhyme-and rea-son to the wild out-doors

It's e-nough for this rest-less war-rior just to be— with you.—
when the heart of this star-crossed voy-ag-er beats in time— with yours.
And can you feel— the love—

— to-night?— It is where— we are.—

It's e-nough— for this wide-eyed— wan-der-er that we got this far.—

And can you feel— the love— to-night,—

how it's laid— to rest? It's e-nough— to make

kings— and— vag-a-bonds— be-lieve the ver-y best.

1

2

It's e-nough— to make kings— and— vag-a-bonds— be-lieve the ver-y best.—

BUT IT'S ALRIGHT

Words and Music by JEROME L. JACKSON
and PIERRE TUBBS

CAN'T HELP FALLING IN LOVE

Words and Music by GEORGE DAVID WEISS,
HUGO PERETTI and LUIGI CREATORE

(They Long to Be)
CLOSE TO YOU

Lyric by HAL DAVID
Music by BURT BACHARACH

We present a useful solo edition of the song, rather than The Carpenter's specialty arrangement.

COME MONDAY

Words and Music by
JIMMY BUFFETT

COPACABANA
(At the Copa)

Words by BRUCE SUSSMAN and JACK FELDMAN
Music by BARRY MANILOW

CROCODILE ROCK

Words and Music by ELTON JOHN
and BERNIE TAUPIN

CRYING

Words and Music by ROY ORBISON
and JOE MELSON

ev - en more__ than I did be - fore, but dar - ling, what can I do?_____ For you

(Oo,   oo,   oo)   (Ah)

don't love me and I'll al - ways be_____ cry - ing o - ver you,__

(Ah)_____   (Ah)_____   (Ah)_____

cry - ing o - ver you.__ Yes, now you're gone and from_____ this mo - ment

(Ah)_____   (Oo)_____   (Oo)_____

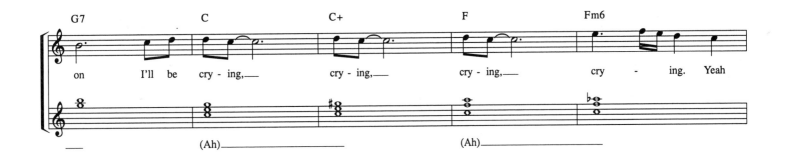

on I'll be cry - ing,__ cry - ing,__ cry - ing,__ cry - ing. Yeah

__   (Ah)_____   (Ah)_____

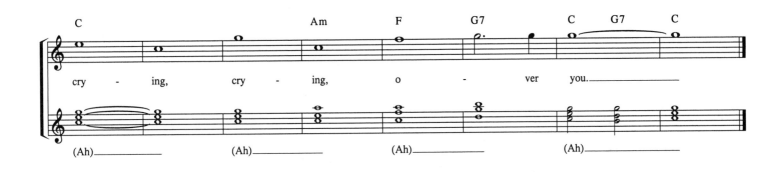

cry - ing, cry - ing, o - ver you._____

(Ah)_____   (Ah)_____   (Ah)_____   (Ah)_____

DAYDREAM BELIEVER

Words and Music by
JOHN STEWART

DREAM BABY
(How Long Must I Dream)

Words and Music by
CINDY WALKER

DON'T BE CRUEL
(To a Heart That's True)

Words and Music by OTIS BLACKWELL
and ELVIS PRESLEY

DON'T LET ME BE LONELY TONIGHT

Words and Music by
JAMES TAYLOR

DREAM LOVER

Words and Music by
BOBBY DARIN

'50s Rock

Ev - 'ry night I hope and pray_____ a dream lov - er will come my way,_
Dream lov - er, where are you,_____ with a love, oh, so true,_
Dream lov - er, un - til then_____ I'll go to sleep and dream a - gain._

a girl to hold in my arms_____ and know the mag - ic of her charms,
and a hand that I can hold_____ to feel you near when I grow old? } be - cause I
That's the on - ly thing to do_____ un - til my lov - er's dreams come true,_ }

want a girl to call_____ my own,_____ I want a

dream_ lov - er so I don't have to dream a - lone.

Some - day, I don't know how,_

I hope you'll hear my plea._ Some - way, I don't know how,_

D.S. al Coda

she'll bring her love to me._

CODA

DUKE OF EARL

Words and Music by EARL EDWARDS,
EUGENE DIXON and BERNICE WILLIAMS

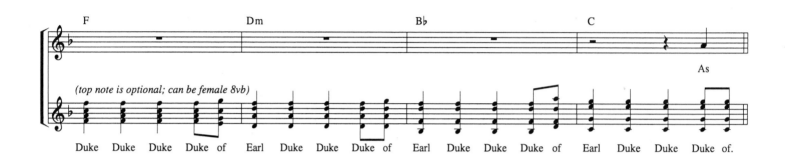

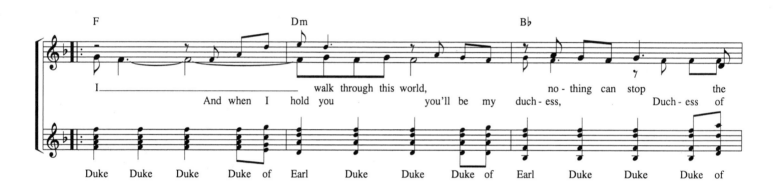

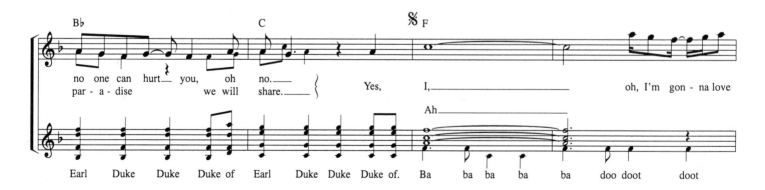

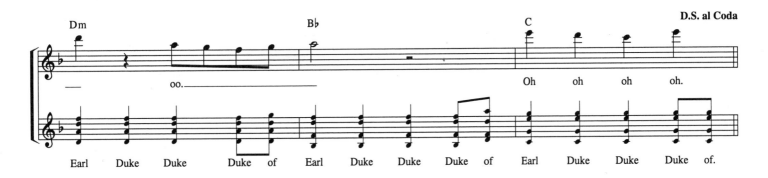

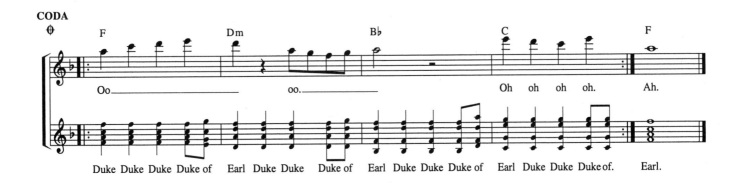

DUST IN THE WIND

Words and Music by
KERRY LIVGREN

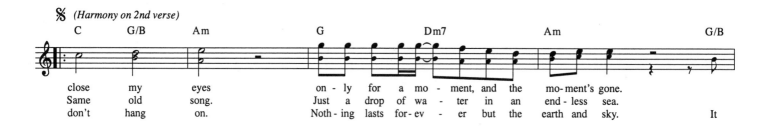

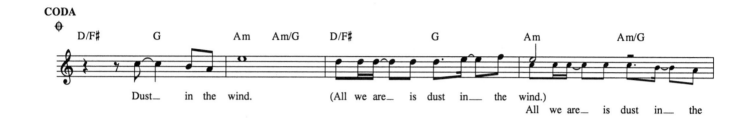

CODA

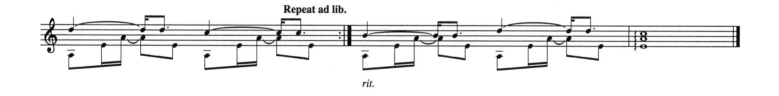

ENDLESS LOVE

Words and Music by
LIONEL RICHIE

Moderately slow

My love,— there's on - ly
Two hearts,— two hearts that

you in my life,— the on - ly thing that's right.— My
beat as— one;— our lives have just be - gun.— For -

first— love,— you're ev - 'ry breath that I take,— you're ev - 'ry
ev - er,— I'll hold you close in my arms,— I can't re -

step I make.— And I, I— want to share all my
sist your charms. And love, I'll be a fool for

love—————— with you, no one else—— will— do.
you—— I'm—— sure; you— know I don't mind.——

And your eyes,— they tell me how much you— care.
'Cause you,— you mean the world to— me.

—— Oh,——— yes, you will al - ways be
—— Oh, I know I've found—— in you

my end - less love.——
my end - less

EVERY BREATH YOU TAKE

Written and Composed by
STING

Since you've gone_ I been lost_ with - out_ a trace, I dream at night I can on -

- ly see_ your face. I look a-round but it's you I can't_ re-place, I feel so cold and I

long for your_ em-brace. I keep cry-ing, "Ba - by, ba - by, please."_

Doo - duh, doo - duh, doo - duh, doo - duh,

doo - duh, doo - duh, doo - duh.

D.S. al Coda

Oh, can't you

CODA

Ev - 'ry move_ you make, ev - 'ry step_ you take, I'll be watch-ing you.

I'll be watch - ing

(Ev-'ry breath you take, ev-'ry move_ you make, ev-'ry bond_ you break, ev-'ry step_ you take,
(ev-'ry move you make, ev-'ry vow_ you break, ev-'ry smile_ you fake, ev-'ry claim you stake,

you.   I'll be watch - ing

ev-'ry sin - gle day, ev-'ry word_ you say, ev-'ry game_ you play, ev-'ry night_ you stay,)

you.   I'll be watch - ing

you. (Instr.)

EVERYTHING I OWN

Words and Music by
DAVID GATES

Moderate

You shel-tered me____ from harm,

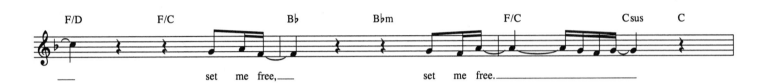

kept me warm,____ kept me warm._____ You gave my life____ to me,

____ set me free,____ set me free._____

The fin-est years I ev-er knew____ were all____ the years I had____ with you.
No-bod-y else could ev-er know____ the part____ of me____ that can't let go.____

_____ And I would give an - y-thing____ I own,____ give up my life,

_____ my heart,____ my home.____ I would give ev - 'ry-thing____ I own____

To Coda

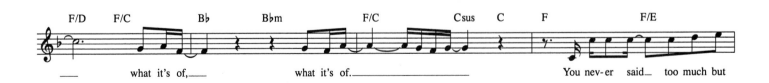

____ just to have____ you back a-gain.____ You taught me____ how to love,

____ what it's of,____ what it's of._____ You nev-er said____ too much but

still you showed the way,— and I knew— from watch - ing you.—

CODA

— Is there some - one you know,— you're lov - ing them so,— but

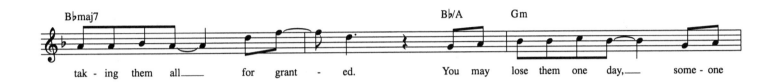

tak - ing them all— for grant - ed. You may lose them one day,— some - one

takes them a - way— and they don't— hear the words you long— to say.— I would give an -

- y - thing— I own,— give up my life,— my heart,— my home..

— I would give ev - 'ry - thing— I own— just to have

— you back a - gain,— just to touch— you once a - gain.—

EVERYTIME YOU GO AWAY

Words and Music by
DARYL HALL

G#dim / D / Bm

ev - 'ry-thing go-ing on and on and on. Ev - 'ry-time you go a - way,

Em / A / D / **Repeat ad lib.**

you take a piece of me with you. Ev - 'ry-time you go.

THE FIRST TIME EVER I SAW YOUR FACE

Words and Music by
EWAN MacCOLL

Slowly

Am7 Bm/F# Cmaj7 Am7 / G / F / G

Am / D7 / G

The first time ev - er I saw your face,
The first time ev - er I kissed your mouth,
The first time ev - er I lay with you

Em / Bm / C

I thought the sun rose in your eyes, and the moon
I felt the earth move in my hand, like the trem -
and felt your heart so close to mine, and I knew

D / D7 / G / **To Coda** / F

and the stars were the gifts you gave to the dark
- bling heart of a cap - tive bird that was there
our joy would fill the earth

1 G / **2** G / **D.S. al Coda**

and the end of the skies.
at my com - mand, my love.

CODA

G / F / G

and last till the end of time, my love.

Am / G/D / D / Am7 Bm/F# Cmaj7 Am7 G

The first time ev - er I saw your face,

F / G / F / G

your face, your face, your face.

FIELDS OF GOLD

Written and Composed by
STING

Flowing, moderately

You'll re-

mem- ber me when the west wind moves up- on the fields of bar- ley. You'll for-
stay with me, will you be my love a- mong the fields of bar- ley? We'll for-

get the sun in his jeal- ous sky as we walk in fields of gold.
get the sun in his jeal- ous sky as we lie in fields of gold.

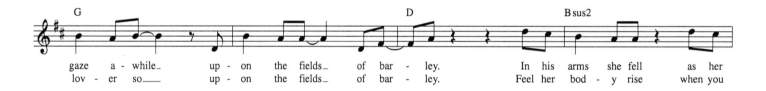

So she took her love for to
See the west wind move like a

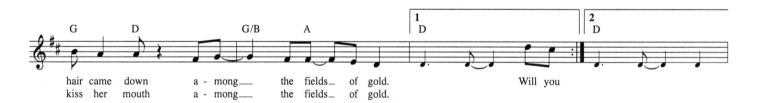

gaze a- while up- on the fields of bar- ley. In his arms she fell as her
lov- er so up- on the fields of bar- ley. Feel her bod- y rise when you

hair came down a- mong the fields of gold. Will you
kiss her mouth a- mong the fields of gold.

I nev- er made prom- is- es light- ly and there have been some that I've bro- ken,

but I swear in the days still left we'll walk in fields of gold.

FIRE AND RAIN

Words and Music by
JAMES TAYLOR

GET BACK

Words and Music by JOHN LENNON
and PAUL McCARTNEY

Jo Jo was a man who thought he was a lon-er, but he knew it could-n't last. Jo
Instrumental
Sweet Lor-et-ta Mar-tin thought she was a wom-an, but she was an-oth-er man. All
Instrumental

Jo left his home in Tuc-son Ar-i-zo-na, for some Cal-i-for-nia grass.
the girls a-round her say she's got it com-ing, but she gets it while she can. Get back!

Get back! Get back to where you once be-longed. Get back!

Get back! Get back to where you once be-longed. *Spoken:* Get back, Jo Jo.

Get back, Loretta, your momma's waitin' for you
Wearin' her high heel shoes and a low neck sweater.
Get back home, Loretta.

GET UP STAND UP

Words and Music by BOB MARLEY
and PETER TOSH

GLORIA

Words and Music by
VAN MORRISON

GOOD LOVIN'

Words and Music by RUDY CLARK
and ARTHUR RESNICK

GOT MY MIND SET ON YOU

Words and Music by
RUDY CLARK

GREAT BALLS OF FIRE

Words and Music by OTIS BLACKWELL
and JACK HAMMER

HE DON'T LOVE YOU
(Like I Love You)

Words and Music by JERRY BUTLER,
CALVIN CARTER and CURTIS MAYFIELD

HAPPY TOGETHER

Words and Music by GARRY BONNER
and ALAN GORDON

Steady, solid beat

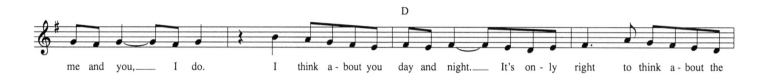

I-mag-ine

me and you,___ I do.   I think a-bout you day and night.___ It's on-ly right to think a-bout the

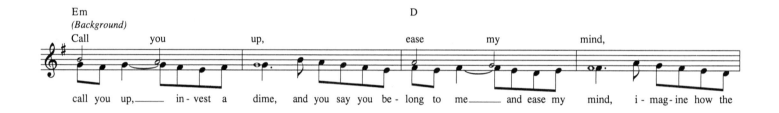

girl you love,___ and hold her tight, so hap-py to-geth-er.___   If I should

Call   you   up,   ease   my   mind,
call you up,___ in-vest a dime, and you say you be-long to me___ and ease my mind, i-mag-ine how the

ver - y   fine.
world could be___ so ver-y fine, so hap-py to-geth-er.___   (Instrumental)

I   can see me lov-in' no-bod-y but   you   for all my   life.___
(Ah)___

When you're with me, ba-by, the skies___ will be   blue   for all my   life.___
(Ah)___

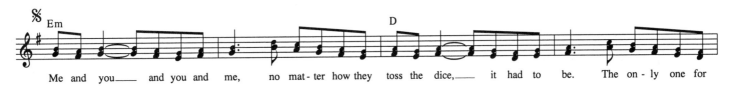

Me and you___ and you and me, no mat-ter how they toss the dice,___ it had to be. The on-ly one for

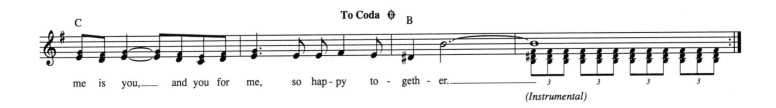

me is you,___ and you for me, so hap-py to - geth - er.___ (Instrumental)

(Instr.)

Ba ba ba ba ba ba ba ba ba ba ba.___

Ba ba ba ba ba ba ba ba ba ba ba.___

CODA

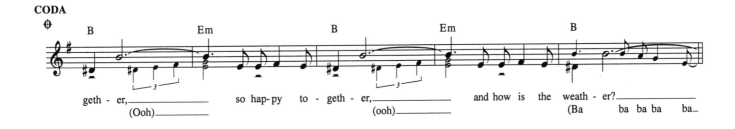

geth - er, (Ooh)___ so hap-py to - geth - er, (ooh)___ and how is the weath - er?___ (Ba ba ba ba ba___

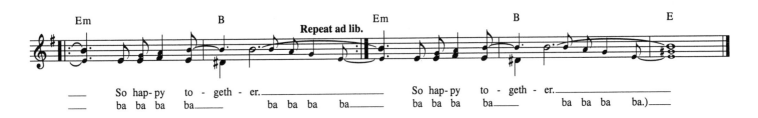

___ So hap-py to - geth - er.___ So hap-py to - geth - er.___
___ ba ba ba ba___ ba ba ba ba___ ba ba ba ba___ ba ba ba ba.)___

HEARTBREAK HOTEL

Words and Music by MAE BOREN AXTON,
TOMMY DURDEN and ELVIS PRESLEY

HERE, THERE AND EVERYWHERE

Words and Music by JOHN LENNON
and PAUL McCARTNEY

HEAVEN IN YOUR EYES

from the Paramount Motion Picture TOP GUN

Words and Music by PAUL DEAN, MIKE RENO,
JOHN DEXTER and MAE MOORE

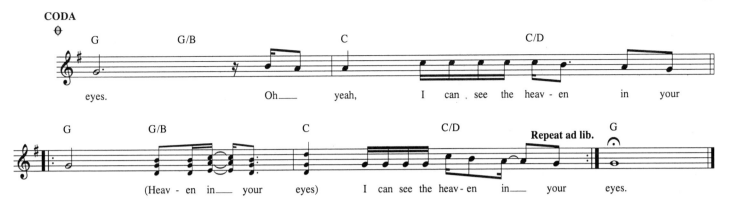

HOUND DOG

Words and Music by JERRY LEIBER
and MIKE STOLLER

I WANT TO HOLD YOUR HAND

Words and Music by JOHN LENNON
and PAUL McCARTNEY

I WILL

Words and Music by JOHN LENNON
and PAUL McCARTNEY

(I'VE HAD) THE TIME OF MY LIFE
from DIRTY DANCING

Words and Music by DONALD MARKOWITZ,
JOHN DeNICOLA and FRANKIE PREVITE

63

I SHOT THE SHERIFF

Words and Music by
BOB MARLEY

IF

Words and Music by
DAVID GATES

IMAGINE

Words and Music by
JOHN LENNON

IN MY LIFE

Words and Music by JOHN LENNON
and PAUL McCARTNEY

IT'S STILL ROCK AND ROLL TO ME

Words and Music by
BILLY JOEL

Moderately fast

JUST ONCE

Words by CYNTHIA WEIL
Music by BARRY MANN

JUST THE WAY YOU ARE

Words and Music by
BILLY JOEL

Let's Hang On

Words and Music by BOB CREWE,
SANDY LINZER and DENNY RANDELL

LET'S HANG ON - Background vocals

hang on, hang on,   doot, doot, doot.   Ah,   Ah,

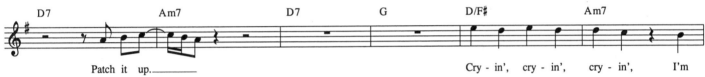

ah.   ah.   ah.

I sure love you like no one, no one. Patch it up.

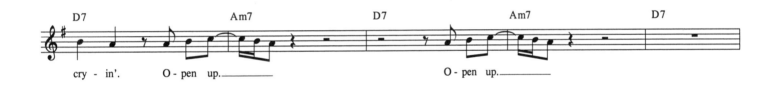

Patch it up.   Cry - in', cry - in', cry - in', I'm

cry - in'. O - pen up.   O - pen up.

D.S. al Fine

Don't you go.   Oh, no, no,   think it o - ver and stay - ay. Let's hang on

THE LOCO-MOTION

Words and Music by GERRY GOFFIN
and CAROLE KING

Moderately

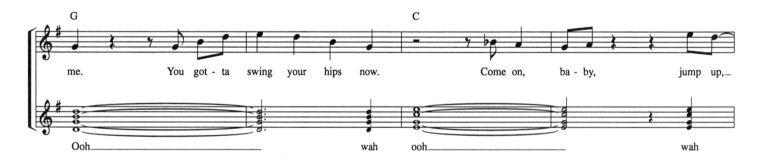

LONG COOL WOMAN
(In a Black Dress)

Words and Music by ALLAN CLARKE,
ROGER COOK and ROGER GREENAWAY

With just one look___ I was a bad mess 'cause that long___

cool___ wom - an had it all.___

CODA

___ Well, the D.___ A. was pump - ing my left___ hand and she was,___

___ was a - hold - ing my right. Well, I told___ her don't get scared 'cause you're

gon - na be spared.___ Well, I'm gon - na be for - giv - en 'cause I wan - na spend my liv - ing with a

long cool___ wom - an in a black dress. Just a five - nine___ beau - ti - ful tall.___

With just one look___ I was a bad man 'cause that long___

___ cool wom - an had it all.___ Get it on.___

Get it on.___ Get it on.___

LOVE SNEAKIN' UP ON YOU

Words and Music by JIMMY SCOTT
and TOM SNOW

Moderate tempo

Rain - y night, I'm all a - lone,_ sit - ting here wait - ing for your
No - where on earth_ for your heart to hide_ once love comes sneak - in' up on

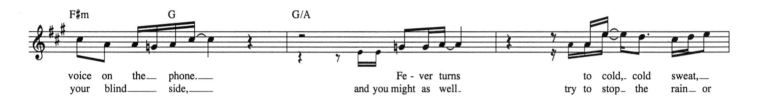

voice on the_ phone.__ Fe - ver turns to cold,_ cold sweat,
your blind_____ side,_____ and you might as well__ try to stop_ the rain_ or

think - ing a - bout_____ the things we_ ain't done yet.__ (1.) Tell me now, I've got to
stand in the tracks_____ of a run - a - way train.__ (2.) You just can't fight it, when a
(D.S.) *Guitar solo*

know. Do you feel the same? Do you just light up at the men - tion of my name?_
thing is_ meant to be._ So come on, let's fin - ish what you start - ed with me._
Solo ends

Don't wor - ry, ba - by. It ain't noth - ing new.__ That's just love_ sneak - in'

up on you.__ If your whole world is shak - in'_ and you feel like_ I do,_

that's just love___ sneak-in' up on you. Hey, hey.___

up on you.___ Hey,_____ yeah.

up on you.___ Well,_____ Don't wor-ry, ba-by. It ain't noth-ing new.___

That's just love___ sneak-in' up on you.___ If your whole world is shak-in'___ and you

feel like___ I do,___ that's just love___ sneak-in' up on you.___ Well, now, up on you.___

LIDO SHUFFLE

Words and Music by BOZ SCAGGS
and DAVID PAICH

MAYBE BABY

By NORMAN PETTY
and CHARLES HARDIN

MISSING YOU

Words by JOHN WAITE
Music by JOHN WAITE,
CHAS SANDFORD and MARK LEONARD

Medium Rock Ballad

Miss-ing you. Miss-ing you. Miss-ing you. Miss-ing you.

Ev-'ry time I think of you, I al-ways catch my breath. And I'm still

stand-ing here, and you're miles a-way, and I'm won-d'rin' why you left. And there's a

storm that's rag-in' through my fro-zen heart to-night. I hear your

name in cer-tain cir-cles, and it al-ways makes me smile. I spend my

time think-in' a-bout you, and it's al-most driv-in' me wild. And there's a

heart that's break-in' down this long dis-tance line to-night. I ain't miss-in' you at all

since you've been gone a-way. I ain't miss-in' you,

no mat-ter what I might say. There's a mes-sage in the wi-

-re, and I'm send-ing you this sig-nal to-night. You don't know how des-p'rate

THE NEXT TIME I FALL

Words and Music by PAUL GORDON
and BOBBY CALDWELL

MAYBE I'M AMAZED

Words and Music by
PAUL McCARTNEY

Slowly, with a beat

(Instr.) (arp.)

Ba-by, I'm a-mazed at the way you love me all the time, and may-be I'm a-fraid of the way I love
May-be I'm a-mazed at the way you're with me all the time. May-be I'm a-fraid of the way I need

you. (Bass)
you.

Ba-by, I'm a-mazed at the way you pulled me out of time. You
Ba-by, I'm a-mazed at the way you help me sing my song,

hung me on a line. Ba-by, I'm a-mazed at the way I real-ly need you.
right me when I'm wrong. Ba-by, I'm a-mazed at the way I real-ly need you.

To Coda ⊕

(Bass)

Ba-by, I'm a man, may-be I'm a lone-ly man who's in the mid-dle of some-thing
(Background vocals)
Ah,

that he does-n't real-ly un-der-stand. (Instr.)
ah

Ba-by, I'm a man, and may-be you're the on-ly wom-an who could ev-er help me.
ah,

91

CODA

NEW YORK STATE OF MIND

Words and Music by
BILLY JOEL

Slowly, with a blues feel

(1.) Some folks___ like to get a - way, take a hol - i - day from the neigh-bor-hood,
(2.) I've seen___ all the mov - ie stars in their fan - cy cars and their lim - ou - sines,
(3.,5.) Comes down___ to re - al - i - ty, and it's fine with me 'cause I've let it slide.
(4.) *Instrumental*

hop a flight to Mi - am - i Beach or to Hol - ly - wood.
been high in the Rock - ies___ un - der the ev - er - greens.
Don't care if it's Chi - na-town or on Riv - er - side.

OH, PRETTY WOMAN

Words and Music by ROY ORBISON
and BILL DEES

PLEASE COME TO BOSTON

Words and Music by
DAVE LOGGINS

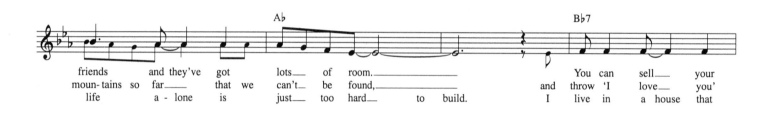

1. Please come to Bos-ton for the spring-time. I'm stay-ing here with some
2. Please come to Den-ver with the snow-fall. We'll move up in-to the
3. Please come to L. A. to live for-ev-er. A Cal-i-for-nia

friends and they've got lots of room. You can sell your
moun-tains so far that we can't be found, and throw 'I love you'
life a-lone is just too hard to build. I live in a house that

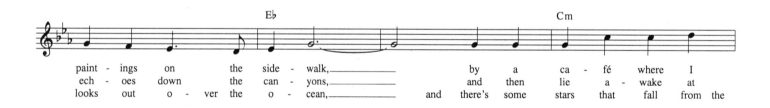

paint-ings on the side-walk, by a ca-fé where I
ech-oes down the can-yons, and then lie a-wake at
looks out o-ver the o-cean, and there's some stars that fall from the

hope to be work-ing soon.
night un-til they come back a-round. Please come to ⎰ Bos-ton, ⎱ she said
sky liv-in' up on the hill. ⎱ Den-ver, ⎰
                                       ⎰ L. A., ⎱

no, but you come home to me. And she said, "Hey,

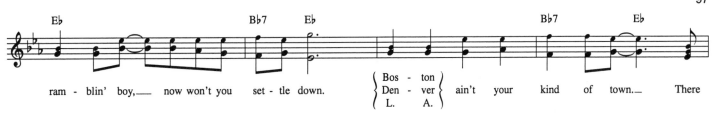

ram - blin' boy,___ now won't you set - tle down. {Bos - ton / Den - ver / L. A.} ain't your kind of town.___ There

ain't no gold___ and there ain't no - bod - y like me._____ I'm the num - ber one fan of the

To Coda ⊕ | 1 | 2

man from Ten - nes - see."_____

Now this

drif - ter's world goes 'round and 'round___ and I doubt___ if it's ev - er gon - na stop. But of

all the dreams I've lost or found, and all___ that I___ ain't got,___ I still need to

D.S. al Coda

lean to some - bod - y I can sing to._____

CODA
⊕

___ "I'm the num - ber one fan of the man___ from Ten - nes - see."_____

ONLY THE LONELY
(Know the Way I Feel)

Words and Music by ROY ORBISON
and JOE MELSON

Sea of Love

Words and Music by GEORGE KHOURY
and PHILIP BAPTISTE

SEPTEMBER

Words and Music by MAURICE WHITE,
AL McKAY and ALLEE WILLIS

Am7 D7 Bm7 Em7 Am7 D7 Bm7 Em7

Ba - de - ya, danc-ing in Sep-tem - ber. Ba - de - ya, (1.,3.) nev - er was a cloud - y day.
(2.,4.) gold-en dreams were shin - y days.

Ba - de - ya, de - ya. 1.-4. Ba - de - ya, de - ya, de - ya.)

1–3
Fmaj7/G

Repeat ad lib.
There was a

4
Fmaj7/G

SHE'S GOT A WAY

Words and Music by
BILLY JOEL

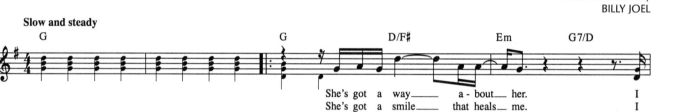

Slow and steady

G G D/F♯ Em G7/D

She's got a way a - bout her. I
She's got a smile that heals me. I

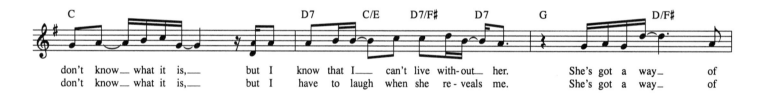

C D7 C/E D7/F♯ D7 G D/F♯

don't know what it is, but I know that I can't live with-out her. She's got a way of
don't know what it is, but I have to laugh when she re-veals me. She's got a way of

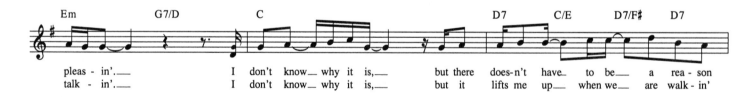

Em G7/D C D7 C/E D7/F♯ D7

pleas - in'. I don't know why it is, but there does-n't have to be a rea - son
talk - in'. I don't know why it is, but it lifts me up when we are walk - in'

1
E♭maj7 Fsus(add2)

2
E♭maj7 Fsus(add2) G

an - y - where.
an - y - where. She

D Am G Gm

comes to me when I'm feel - in' down, in - spires me with - out a sound. She

SIMPLY IRRESISTIBLE

Words and Music by
ROBERT PALMER

How

can it be per-mis-si-ble?
lov-ing is so pow-er-ful.
meth-ods are in-scru-ta-ble!

She
It's
The

com-pro-mise my prin-ci-ple.
sim-ply un-a-void-a-ble.
proof is ir-re-fu-ta-ble.

Yeah, yeah.____
Whoa, whoa.____

That
The
She's

kind of love is myth-i-cal;
trend is ir-re-vers-i-ble,
so com-plete-ly kiss-a-ble,

she's an the-
the wom-
our lives

-y-thing but typ-i-cal.____
-an is in-vin-ci-ble.____
____ are in-di-vis-i-ble.

She's a
She's a
She's a

craze you'd en-dorse; she's a pow-er-ful force. You're o-bliged to con-form,____ when there's no oth-er course. She
nat-u-ral law____ and she leaves me in awe.___ She de-serves the ap-plause. I sur-ren-der be-cause.____ she
craze you'd en-dorse; she's a pow-er-ful force. You're o-bliged to con-form,____ when there's no oth-er course. She

(Drums)

used to look good to me,____ but now I find her____
used to look good to me,____ but now I find her____
used to look good to me,____ but now I find her____

sim-ply ir-re-

sist-i-ble,

sim-ply ir-re-

*Melody line is notated one octave lower than sung.

SO FAR AWAY

Words and Music by
CAROLE KING

Very slow

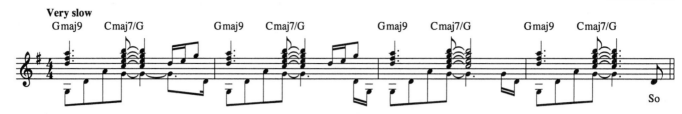

So

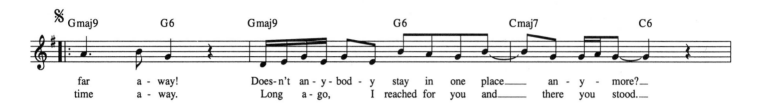

far a - way! Does-n't an - y - bod - y stay in one place____ an - y - more?____
time a - way. Long a - go, I reached for you and____ there you stood.____

It would be so fine to see____ your____ face at my door.____ Does-n't help__ to know you're just
Hold - ing you a - gain could on - ly____ do me____ good.____

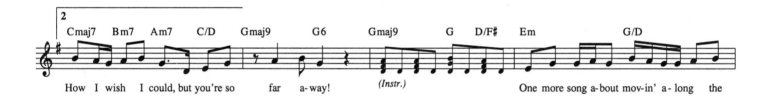

How I wish I could, but you're so far a - way! (Instr.) One more song a - bout mov-in' a - long the

high - way.__ Can't say much of an - y - thing that's new. If I could on - ly work this life out

__ my____ way,_ I'd rath - er spend__ it be - in' close to you.__ But you're so

CODA

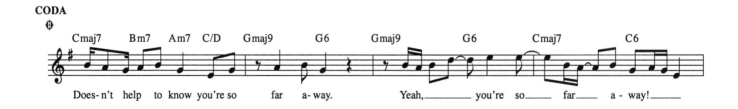

Does-n't help to know you're so far a - way. Yeah,____ you're so____ far a - way!

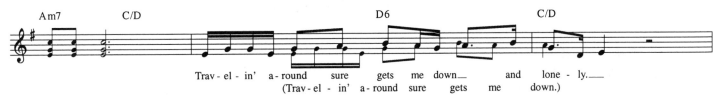

Trav-el-in' a-round sure gets me down___ and lone-ly.___
(Trav-el-in' a-round sure gets me down.)

Noth-in' else to do___ but close my mind. I sure___ hope the road___ don't come to___

___ own___ me.___ There's so man-y dreams___ I've yet to find._____ But you're so

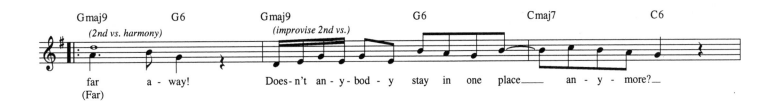

(2nd vs. harmony)   (improvise 2nd vs.)

far   a-way!   Does-n't an-y-bod-y stay in one place___ an-y-more?___
(Far)

Last time rit.   Repeat ad lib.

It would be so fine to see___ your face at my door.___ Does-n't help to know you're so far a-way!

SOME KIND OF WONDERFUL

Words and Music by GERRY GOFFIN
and CAROLE KING

SOMETIMES WHEN WE TOUCH

Words by DAN HILL
Music by BARRY MANN

Slowly, in 2

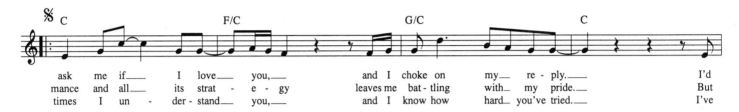

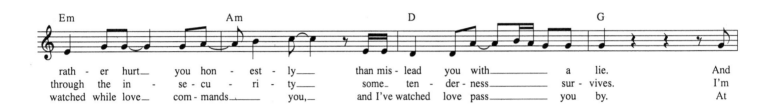

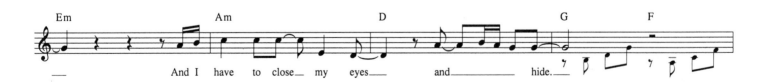

I wan - na hold you till___ I die,___ till we both break down___ and cry.___

To Coda ⊕ | **1**

___ I wan - na hold you till the fear___ in me___ sub - sides.

2

Ro - sides. At

times I'd like___ to break___ you and drive___ you to___ your knees.___ At

D.S. al Coda

times I'd like___ to break___ through and hold_ you end - less-ly.___ At

CODA
⊕

sides.___

SOMEWHERE OUT THERE
from AN AMERICAN TAIL

Words and Music by JAMES HORNER,
BARRY MANN and CYNTHIA WEIL

Moderately, with expression

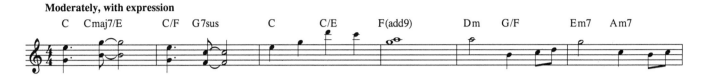

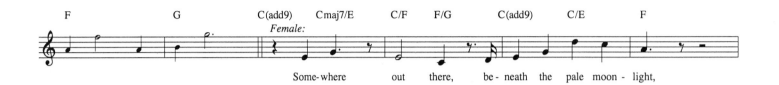

Female: Some-where out there, be - neath the pale moon - light,

some - one's think-in' of me and lov - ing me to - night. *Male:* Some - where out___

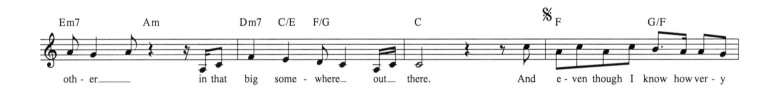

___ there,___ some - one's say - ing a prayer___ that we'll find one an -

oth - er___ in that big some - where___ out___ there. And e - ven though I know how ver - y

far a - part___ we are,___ it helps to think___ we might be wish - in' on the same___ bright - star. *Female:* And

when the night wind starts to sing a lone - some lull - a - by, it helps to think we're sleep - ing un - der -

neath the same big sky. *Male:* *Female:* Some - where out there, if love can see us

through, then we'll be to - geth - er some-where out there, out where dreams come

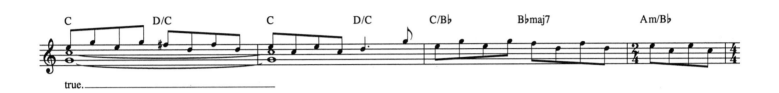

true.

And

love can see us through, then we'll be to - geth - er some-where out there, out

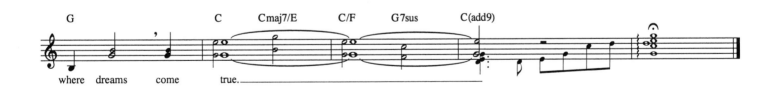

where dreams come true.

STAND BY ME

Words and Music by BEN E. KING,
JERRY LEIBER and MIKE STOLLER

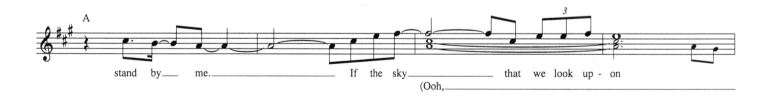

STEAMROLLER
(Steamroller Blues)

Words and Music by
JAMES TAYLOR

TIME AFTER TIME

Words and Music by CYNDI LAUPER
and ROB HYMAN

TEARS IN HEAVEN

Words and Music by ERIC CLAPTON
and WILL JENNINGS

Moderately relaxed tempo

Would you know my name_____ if I saw you in heav - en?
Would you hold my hand_____ if I saw you in heav - en?
Would you know my name_____ if I saw you in heav - en?

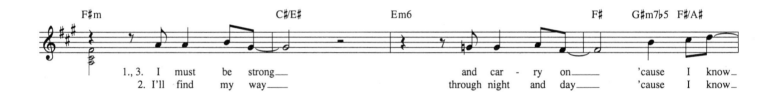

Would it be the same_____ if I saw you in heav - en?
Would you help me stand_____ if I saw you in heav - en?
Would you be the same_____ if I saw you in heav - en?

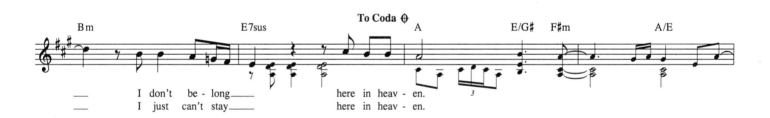

1., 3. I must be strong_____ and car - ry on_____ 'cause I know_____
2. I'll find my way_____ through night and day_____ 'cause I know_____

_____ I don't be - long_____ here in heav - en.
_____ I just can't stay_____ here in heav - en.

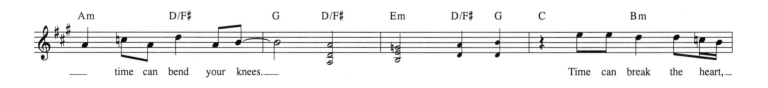

Time can bring you down,_____ time can bend your knees._____ Time can break the heart,_____

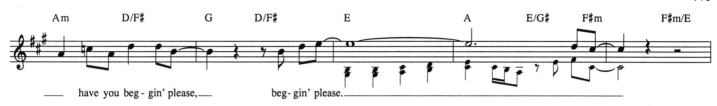

have you beg-gin' please,___ beg-gin' please._____

Be - yond the door___

there's peace, I'm sure.___ And I know___ there'll be no more___ tears in heav-

en.

D.S. al Coda

CODA

en.

TELL IT LIKE IT IS

Words and Music by GEORGE DAVIS
and LEE DIAMOND

If___ you___ want___ some-thing to play___ with,___ go and find___ your-self a

toy.___ Ba-by, my time___ is too ex-pen-sive,

and I'm not___ a lit-tle boy.___

If you are se-ri-ous,___ don't play with my heart;___ it makes me

fu-ri-ous.___ But if you want me to love you, ba-by, I___

will.___ Girl, you know I will. Tell it like it is.___ Don't be a-

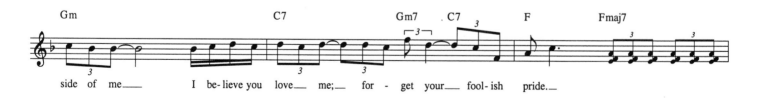

shamed,___ let your con-science___ be your guide.___ But I___ know deep-ly in-

side of me___ I be-lieve you love___ me; for-get your___ fool-ish pride.

THAT'LL BE THE DAY

Words and Music by JERRY ALLISON,
NORMAN PETTY and BUDDY HOLLY

THATꞋLL BE THE DAY - Background vocals

THAT'S ALL RIGHT MAMA

Words and Music by
ARTHUR CRUDUP

Rockabilly

Well,

that's all right, ma - ma. That's all right for you. That's

all right to ma - ma, just an - y way you do, but that's all

right. That's all right. That's all right now,

ma - ma, an - y way you do. Well, ma -

- ma she done told me. Pa - pa done told me, too. Son,
leav - in' town now, ba - by. I'm leav - in' town for sure. Well,

that gal you're fool - in' with, she ain't no good for you, but that's all
then you won't be both - ered with me hang - in' 'round your door.

right. That's all right. That's all right now,

THAT'S THE WAY OF THE WORLD

Words and Music by MAURICE WHITE,
CHARLES STEPNEY and VERDINE WHITE

Hearts of fire cre-ates love de-sire, take you high and high-er to the world you be-long. Hearts of fire cre-ates love de-sire, high and high-er to your place on the throne. We come to-geth-er on this spe-cial day, sing our mes-sage loud and clear, mm. Look-ing back, we've touched on sor-row-ful days. Fu-ture pass, they dis-ap-pear. You will find peace of mind if you look way down in your heart and soul. Ah, don't hes-i-tate 'cause the world seems cold. Stay young at heart 'cause you're nev-er, nev-er old. (nev-er, nev-er, nev-er, nev-er, nev-er, yeah)

THIS MASQUERADE

Words and Music by
LEON RUSSELL

TIME WON'T LET ME

Words and Music by CHET KELLY
and TOM KING

TUTTI FRUTTI

Words and Music by LITTLE RICHARD PENNIMAN
and DOROTHY La BOSTRIE

TWIST AND SHOUT

Words and Music by BERT RUSSELL
and PHIL MEDLEY

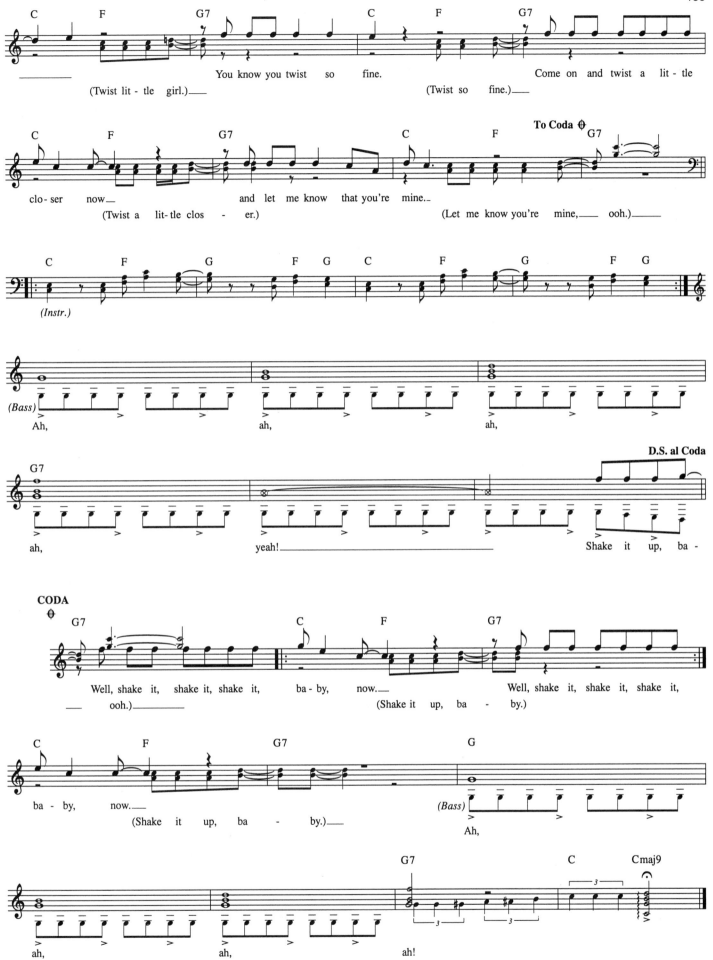

UNCHAINED MELODY

Lyric by HY ZARET
Music by ALEX NORTH

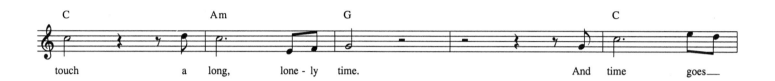

me,_____ wait for me." I'll be____ com-ing home,____ wait for me. Oh, my____

love, my dar - ling, I've hun-gered, hun - gered____ for your touch a long, lone - ly

time. And time goes____ by so slow - ly, and

time can do so much. Are____ you still mine?_____ I_____

need_____ your____ love. I, I need your love. God speed your love

to me.

UNDER THE BOARDWALK

Words and Music by ARTIE RESNICK
and KENNY YOUNG

*Background "Ooh," 2nd verse.

UP ON THE ROOF

Words and Music by GERRY GOFFIN
and CAROLE KING

UP WHERE WE BELONG

from the Paramount Picture AN OFFICER AND A GENTLEMAN

Words by WILL JENNINGS
Music by BUFFY SAINTE-MARIE and JACK NITZSCHE

moun - tain high.   Love lift us up where we be-long,_____   far from the

_____   Love lift us up.   Oh._____

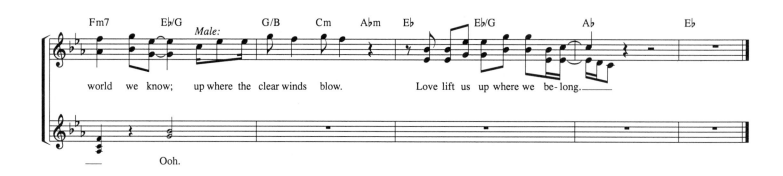

world we know; up where the clear winds blow.   Love lift us up where we be-long._____

_____ Ooh.

WALK AWAY RENEE

Words and Music by MIKE BROWN,
TONY SANSONE and BOB CALILLI

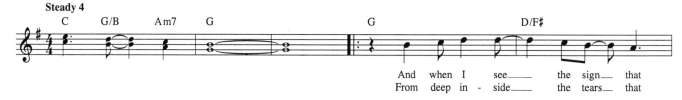

And when I   see____   the sign____   that
From deep in - side____   the tears____   that

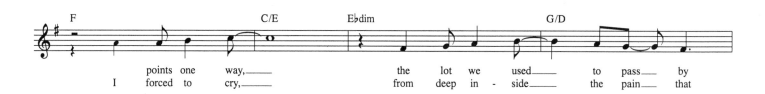

points one   way,_____   the lot we used____ to pass   by
I forced to cry,_____   from deep in - side____ the pain____ that

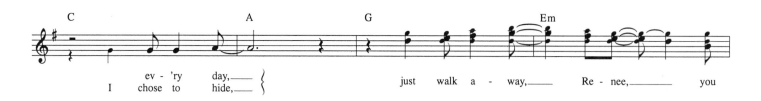

ev - 'ry   day,_____ {   just walk a - way,_____   Re - nee,_____   you
I chose to hide,_____ {

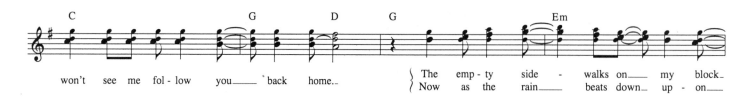

won't see me fol - low you___ back home.___   { The   emp - ty   side - walks on____ my   block
                                                        { Now   as the   rain____ beats down up - on____

___ are not the same, ___ you're not to blame.___

___ my wear-y heart,___ for me it cries.___

Just walk a-way,___ Re-nee,___ you won't___ see me fol-low you___

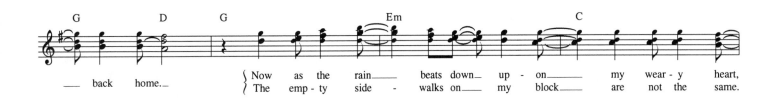

___ back home.___ Now as the rain___ beats down___ up-on___ my wear-y heart,

The emp-ty side-walks on___ my block___ are not the same.

___ for me it cries.___ Your name and mine___

You're not to blame.

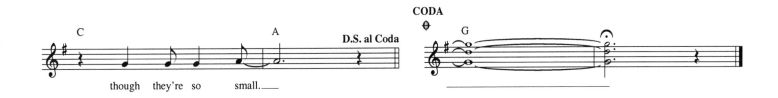

___ in-side___ a heart up-on a wall___ still finds a way___ to haunt___ me,

though they're so small.___

WAY OVER YONDER

Words and Music by
CAROLE KING

Gospel Blues

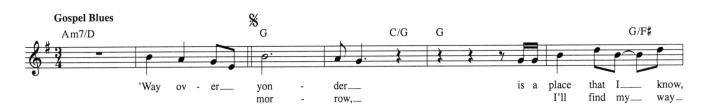

'Way ov-er yon-der___ is a place that I___ know,
mor-row,___ I'll find my way

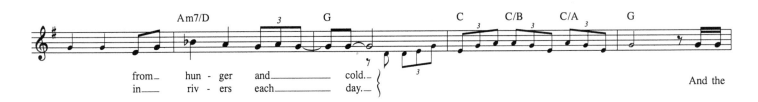

where I can find___ shel-ter___
to the land where the___ hon-ey runs

from___ hun-ger and___ cold.
in___ riv-ers each___ day. And the

sweet tast-in' good___ life___ is so eas - i-ly found.___

'Way o-ver yon-der,___ that's where I'm___ bound.

I know___ when I get there,___ the

first thing I'll see___ is the sun___ shin-ing gold-en,___

shin-in' right down on___ me.___ Then

trou - ble's gon - na lose_____ me,_____ wor - ry leave_ me be - hind,_____

_____ and I'll stand up proud - ly_____ in true peace of

mind. Talk - in' 'bout a, talk - in' 'bout a - way o - ver yon - der__

is a place I have seen.__ It's a gar - den of

wis - dom_ from_ some long_ a - go___ dream._____

_____ May - be___ to -

WHY

Words and Music by
ANNIE LENNOX

WE JUST DISAGREE

Words and Music by
JIM KRUEGER

WILD THING

Words and Music by
CHIP TAYLOR

WONDERFUL TONIGHT

Words and Music by
ERIC CLAPTON

WOOLY BULLY

Words and Music by
DOMINGO SAMUDIO

WILL YOU LOVE ME TOMORROW
(Will You Still Love Me Tomorrow)

Words and Music by GERRY GOFFIN
and CAROLE KING

Will you still love me to-mor-row?   Will you still love me to-mor-
- row?

YESTERDAY

Words and Music by JOHN LENNON
and PAUL McCARTNEY

Moderately, with expression

Yes-ter-day,——
Sud-den-ly,——

all my trou-bles seemed so far a-way.——   Now it looks as though they're
I'm not half the man— I used to be.   There's a shad-ow hang-ing

here to stay.——   Oh, I be-lieve—— in yes-ter-day.——
o-ver me.——   Oh, yes-ter-day—— came sud-den-ly.——

Why she had to go I don't know, she would-n't say.——

I said some-thing wrong, now I long for yes-ter-day.

Yes-ter-day,——   love was such an eas-y game to play.——

Now I need a place to hide a-way.——   Oh, I be-lieve—— in

yes-ter-day.——   Mm mm mm mm mm.——

YOU'VE GOT A FRIEND

Words and Music by
CAROLE KING

YOU'VE LOST THAT LOVIN' FEELIN'

Words and Music by BARRY MANN,
CYNTHIA WEIL and PHIL SPECTOR

*Solo singers are called I and II.

YOUR SONG

Words and Music by ELTON JOHN
and BERNIE TAUPIN

THE ULTIMATE COLLECTION OF
FAKE BOOKS

The Ultimate Fake Book – 2nd Edition

Over 1200 songs, including: All I Ask of You • All the Things You Are • Always • And So It Goes • Autumn in New York • Blue Skies • Body and Soul • Call Me Irresponsible • Can't Help Falling in Love • Caravan • Easter Parade • Endless Love • Heart and Soul • The Impossible Dream • Isn't It Romantic? • The Lady Is a Tramp • Lay Down Sally • Let's Fall in Love • Moon River • My Funny Valentine • Piano Man • Roxanne • Satin Doll • Sophisticated Lady • Speak Low • Splish Splash • Strawberry Fields Forever • Tears in Heaven • A Time for Us (Love Theme from Romeo & Juliet) • Unforgettable • When I Fall in Love • When You Wish upon a Star • and hundreds more!

00240024 C Edition $45.00
00240025 E♭ Edition $45.00
00240026 B♭ Edition $45.00

Best Fake Book Ever – 2nd Edition

More than 1000 songs from all styles of music, including: All My Loving • American Pie • At the Hop • The Birth of the Blues • Cabaret • Can You Feel the Love Tonight • Don't Cry for Me Argentina • Dust in the Wind • Fever • Free Bird • From a Distance • The Girl from Ipanema • Hello, Dolly! • Hey Jude • I Heard It Through the Grapevine • The Keeper of the Stars • King of the Road • Longer • Misty • Route 66 • Sentimental Journey • Somebody • Somewhere in Time • Song Sung Blue • Spanish Eyes • Spinning Wheel • Take the "A" Train • Unchained Melody • We Will Rock You • What a Wonderful World • Wooly Bully • Y.M.C.A. • You're So Vain • and hundreds more.

00290239 C Edition $45.00
00240083 B♭ Edition $45.00
00240084 E♭ Edition $45.00

The Ultimate Pop/Rock Fake Book – 3rd Edition

Over 500 pop standards and contemporary hits, including: Addicted To Love • Ain't No Mountain High Enough • All Shook Up • Another One Bites The Dust • Can You Feel The Love Tonight • Crocodile Rock • Crying • Don't Know Much • Dust in the Wind • Earth Angel • Every Breath You Take • Have I Told You Lately • Hero • Hey Jude • Hold My Hand • Imagine • Layla • The Loco-Motion • Maggie May • Me and Bobby McGee • Mission: Impossible Theme • Oh, Pretty Woman • On Broadway • The Power of Love • Save the Best for Last • Spinning Wheel • Stand by Me • Stayin' Alive • Tears in Heaven • True Colors • The Twist • Vision Of Love • What's Going On • A Whole New World • Wild Thing • Wooly Bully • Yesterday • You've Lost That Lovin' Feelin' • and many more!

00240099 $35.00

The Ultimate Jazz Fake Book

Over 625 jazz classics spanning more than nine decades and representing all the styles of jazz. Includes: All of Me • All The Things You Are • Basin Street Blues • Birdland • Desafinado •Don't Get Around Much Anymore • A Foggy Day •I Concentrate On You •In The Mood • Take The "A" Train • Yardbird Suite • and many more!

00240079 C Edition $39.95
00240081 E♭ Edition $39.95
00240080 B♭ Edition $39.95

The Ultimate Broadway Fake Book - 4th Edition

More than 670 show-stoppers from over 200 shows! Includes: Ain't Misbehavin' • All I Ask Of You • As If We Never Said Goodbye • Bewitched • Camelot • Memory • Don't Cry For Me Argentina • Edelweiss • I Dreamed A Dream • If I Were A Rich Man • Oklahoma • People • Seasons Of Love • Send In The Clowns • Someone • What I Did For Love • and more.

00240046 $39.95

The Classical Fake Book

An unprecedented, amazingly comprehensive reference of over 650 classical themes and melodies for all classical music lovers. Includes everything from Renaissance music to Vivaldi and Mozart to Mendelssohn. Lyrics in the original language are included when appropriate. Also features a composer "timeline."

00240044 $24.95

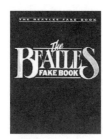

The Beatles Fake Book

200 songs including: All My Loving • And I Love Her • Back In The USSR • Can't Buy Me Love • Day Tripper • Eight Days A Week • Eleanor Rigby • Help! • Here Comes The Sun • Hey Jude • Let It Be • Michelle • Penny Lane • Revolution • Yesterday • and many more.

00240069 $25.00

The Ultimate Country Fake Book

Over 700 super country hits, including: Achy Breaky Heart • Act Naturally • The Battle Hymn Of Love • Boot Scootin' Boogie • The Chair • Friends In Low Places • Grandpa (Tell Me 'Bout The Good Old Days) • Islands In The Stream • Jambalaya • Love Without End, Amen • No One Else On Earth • Okie From Muskogee • She Believes In Me • Stand By Me • What's Forever For • and more.

00240049 $35.00

Wedding & Love Fake Book

Over 400 classic and contemporary songs, including: All For Love • All I Ask Of You • Anniversary Song • Ave Maria • Can You Feel The Love Tonight • Endless Love • Forever And Ever, Amen • Forever In Love • I Wanna Be Loved • It Could Happen To You • Misty • Saving All My Love • So In Love • Through The Years • Vision Of Love • and more.

00240041 $24.95

The Irving Berlin Fake Book

Over 150 Berlin songs, including: Alexander's Ragtime Band • Always • Blue Skies • Easter Parade • God Bless America • Happy Holiday • Heat Wave • I've Got My Love To Keep Me Warm • Puttin' On The Ritz • There's No Business Like Show Business • White Christmas • and many more.

00240043 $19.95

The Ultimate Christmas Fake Book - 3rd Edition

More than 200 holiday tunes, including: Blue Christmas • The Chipmunk Song • Frosty The Snowman • I Saw Mommy Kissing Santa Claus • I'll Be Home For Christmas • Jingle Bells • Rudolph, The Red-Nosed Reindeer • Silent Night • Silver Bells • and more!

00240045 $17.95

Gospel's Best – Words And Music

The best reference book of gospel music ever compiled! Here's a collection of over 500 of the greatest songs of our time, representing all areas of gospel music.

00240048 $24.95

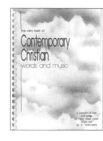

The Very Best Of Contemporary Christian Words & Music

More than 375 songs written and recorded by America's favorite Christian artists, including Amy Grant, Sandi Paul, Petra, Michael W. Smith, Bill & Gloria Gaither and many more.

00240067 $24.95

FOR MORE INFORMATION, SEE YOUR LOCAL MUSIC DEALER, OR WRITE TO:

HAL•LEONARD® CORPORATION

7777 W. BLUEMOUND RD. P.O. BOX 13819 MILWAUKEE, WI 53213
http://www.halleonard.com
Prices, contents and availabilty subject to change without notice

0597

MUSICAL THEATRE COLLECTIONS
FROM HAL LEONARD

BROADWAY BELTER'S SONGBOOK

A great new collection for women singers. All the songs have been chosen especially for this type of voice, and the ranges and keys have been carefully selected. 30 songs, including: Broadway Baby • The Lady Is A Tramp • Everything's Coming Up Roses • I'd Give My Life To You (*Miss Saigon*) • Cabaret. 176 pages.
_____00311608 ....$16.95

THE SINGER'S MUSICAL THEATRE ANTHOLOGY

The most comprehensive collection of Broadway selections ever organized specifically for the singer. Each of the five volumes contains important songs chosen because of their appropriateness to that particular voice type. All selections are in their authentic form, excerpted from the original vocal scores. The songs in *The Singer's Musical Theatre Anthology*, written by such noted composers as Kurt Weill, Richard Rodgers, Stephen Sondheim, and Jerome Kern, are vocal masterpieces ideal for the auditioning, practicing or performing vocalist.

Soprano
46 songs, including: Where Or When • If I Loved You • Goodnight, My Someone • Smoke Gets In Your Eyes • Barbara Song • and many more.
_____00361071 ....$19.95

Mezzo-Soprano/Alto
40 songs, including: My Funny Valentine • I Love Paris • Don't Cry For Me Argentina • Losing My Mind • Send In The Clowns • and many more.
_____00361072 ....$19.95

Tenor
42 songs, including: Stranger In Paradise • On The Street Where You Live • Younger Than Springtime • Lonely House • Not While I'm Around • and more.
_____00361073 ....$19.95

Baritone/Bass
37 songs, including: If Ever I Would Leave You • September Song • The Impossible Dream • Ol' Man River • Some Enchanted Evening • and more.
_____00361074 ....$19.95

Duets
21 songs, including: Too Many Mornings • We Kiss In A Shadow • People Will Say We're In Love • Bess You Is My Woman • Make Believe • more.
_____00361075 ....$16.95

THE SINGER'S MUSICAL THEATRE ANTHOLOGY VOL. 2

More great theatre songs for singers in a continuation of this highly successful and important series, once again compiled and edited by Richard Walters. As is the case with the first volume, these collections are as valuable to the classical singer as they are to the popular and theatre performer.

Soprano, Volume 2
42 songs, including: All Through The Night • And This Is My Beloved • Vilia • If I Were A Bell • Think Of Me.
_____00747066 ....$19.95

Mezzo-Soprano/Alto, Volume 2
44 songs, including: If He Walked Into My Life • The Party's Over • Johnny One Note • Adalaide's Lament • I Hate Men • I Dreamed A Dream.
_____00747031 ....$19.95

Tenor, Volume 2
46 songs, including: Miracle Of Miracles • Sit Down, You're Rockin' The Boat • Giants In The Sky • Bring Him Home • Music Of The Night.
_____00747032 ....$19.95

Baritone/Bass, Volume 2
44 songs, including: Guido's Song from *Nine* • Bye, Bye Baby • I Won't Send Roses • The Surrey With The Fringe On Top • Once In Love With Amy.
_____00747033 ....$19.95

THE ACTOR'S SONGBOOK

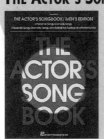

A wonderfully diverse collection of comedy songs, character songs, Vaudeville numbers, dramatic songs, and ballads for the actor who sings. A perfect resource to use for finding an audition song or specialty number. In two editions, one for women, and one for men, with a completely different selection of songs chosen for each edition. Over 50 songs in each book. Women's edition titles include: The Ladies Who Lunch • Cla-wence (Don't Tweat Me So Wough) • Cry Me A River • Shy • The Man That Got Away, and many more. Men's edition includes: Buddy's Blues (from *Follies*) • Doing The Reactionary • How to Handle A Woman • I'm Calm • Reviewing The Situation, many more.
_____00747035 Women's Edition $19.95
_____00747034 Men's Edition $19.95

FOR MORE INFORMATION, SEE YOUR LOCAL MUSIC DEALER, OR WRITE TO:

HAL•LEONARD® CORPORATION
7777 W. BLUEMOUND RD. P.O. BOX 13819 MILWAUKEE, WI 53213

KIDS' BROADWAY SONGBOOK

An unprecedented collection of songs that were originally performed by children on the Broadway stage. A terrific and much needed publication for the thousands of children studying voice. Includes 16 songs for boys and girls: Gary, Indiana (*The Music Man*) • Castle On A Cloud (*Les Miserables*) • Where Is Love? (*Oliver!*) • Tomorrow (*Annie*) • and more.
_____00311609 ....$9.95

MUSICAL THEATRE CLASSICS

A fantastic series featuring the best songs from Broadway classics. Collections are organized by voice type and each book includes recorded piano accompaniments on CD – ideal for practicing. Compiled by Richard Walters, Sue Malmberg, pianist.

Soprano, Volume 1
13 songs, including: Climb Ev'ry Mountain • Falling In Love With Love • Hello, Young Lovers • Smoke Gets In Your Eyes • Wishing You Were Somehow Here Again.
_____00740036 ....$19.95

Soprano, Volume 2
13 more favorites, including: Can't Help Lovin' Dat Man • I Could Have Danced All Night • Show Me • Think Of Me • Till There Was You.
_____00740037 ....$19.95

Mezzo-Soprano/Alto, Volume 1
11 songs, including: Don't Cry For Me Argentina • I Dreamed A Dream • The Lady Is A Tramp • People • and more.
_____00740038 ....$19.95

Mezzo-Soprano/Alto, Volume 2
11 songs, including: Glad To Be Unhappy • Just You Wait • Memory • My Funny Valentine • On My Own • and more.
_____00740039 ....$19.95

Tenor
11 songs, including: All I Need Is A Girl • If You Could See Her • The Music Of The Night • On The Street Where You Live • Younger Than Springtime • and more.
_____00740040 ....$19.95

Baritone/Bass
11 classics, including: If Ever I Would Leave You • If I Loved You • Oh, What A Beautiful Mornin' • Ol' Man River • Try To Remember • and more.
_____00740041 ....$19.95